Let's Celeb...

ELECTION DAY

P9-CQD-265

BY Barbara deRubertis

Kane Press
New York

For activities and resources for this book and others in the HOLIDAYS & HEROES series, visit:
www.kanepress.com/holidays-and-heroes

Text copyright © 2018 by Barbara deRubertis
Photographs/images copyrights: Cover: © Steve Debenport/iStock; cover inset: © Ardesia/Shutterstock; page 1: © Rean Schild/Shutterstock; page 3: © fstop123/iStock; page 4: © Library of Congress, Prints and Photographs Division, LC-DIG-pga-03236; page 5: © Library of Congress, Prints and Photographs Division, LC-USZ62-132545; page 6 left: © Library of Congress, Prints and Photographs Division, LC-DIG-cwpbh-00554; page 6 right: © Library of Congress, Prints and Photographs Division, LC-DIG-pga-07720; page 7: © Library of Congress, Prints and Photographs Division, LC-USZ62-116587; page 8: ©Everett Historical/Shutterstock; page 8 inset: © Library of Congress, Prints and Photographs Division, LC-DIG-hec-36819; page 9: © Library of Congress, Prints and Photographs Division, LOT 3076-11, no. 3630; page 9 inset: © Library of Congress, Prints and Photographs Division, LC-DIG-hec-12073; page 10: © Library of Congress, Prints and Photographs Division, LC-G39-T-8070; page 10 inset: © US Senate Archives/U.S. Senate Historical Office; page 11: © Library of Congress, Prints and Photographs Division, LC-DIG-pprs-00267; pages 12–13: © Library of Congress, Prints and Photographs Division, LC-DIG-ppmsca-08102; page 12 inset: © Library of Congress, Prints and Photographs Division, LC-USZ62-135695; page 14: © Horst Faas/Associated Press; page 14 inset: © Rob Crandall/Shutterstock; page 15: © Alessandro Pietri/Shutterstock; page 16: © wdstock/iStock; page 17: © Wavebreakmedia/Dreamstime.com; page 18: © Jennifer Pieiquen/Dreamstime.com; page 19: © Rob Crandall/Shutterstock; page 20 top: © Lucky Photographer/Shutterstock; page 20 inset 1: © Sean Pavone/Shutterstock; page 20 inset 2: © AG Baxter/Shutterstock; page 21: ©MediaPunch Inc/Alamy Stock Photo; page 22: © Nagel Photography/Shutterstock; page 22 inset: © Art Wager/iStock; page 23: © JrlPhotographer/iStock; page 24: ©Rob Crandall/Shutterstock; page 24 inset: © Eb33/iStock; page 25: © Joseph Sohm/Shutterstock; page 25 inset: Americanspirit/Dreamstime.com; page 26: © Joseph Sohm/Shutterstock; page 27: © Nick Ut/Associated Press; page 28: © Steve Debenport/iStock; page 29: © Paul Hakimata/Dreamstime.com; page 30: © Evenfh/Shutterstock; page 31 left: © Rena Schild/Shutterstock; page 31 right: © Lebrecht Music and Arts Photo Library/Alamy Stock Photo; page 32: © David O Navarro/Shutterstock; back cover: © Steve Debenport/iStock
All due diligence has been conducted in identifying copyright holders and obtaining permissions.

Library of Congress Cataloging-in-Publication Data

Names: deRubertis, Barbara, author.
Title: Let's celebrate election day / by Barbara deRubertis.
Other titles: Let us celebrate election day
Description: New York : Kane Press, 2018. | Series: Holidays & Heroes |
  Audience: Ages: 6-10. | Audience: Grades: 1-4.
Identifiers: LCCN 2018007789 (print) | LCCN 2018015413 (ebook) | ISBN
  9781635920567 (ebook) | ISBN 9781635920543 (reinforced library binding : alk.
  paper) | ISBN 9781635920550 (paperback : alk. paper)
Subjects: LCSH: Elections--United States--History--Juvenile literature. |
  Election Day--History--Juvenile literature.
Classification: LCC JK1978 (ebook) | LCC JK1978 .D47 2018 (print) | DDC
  324.973--dc23
LC record available at https://lccn.loc.gov/2018007789

10 9 8 7 6 5 4 3 2 1

First published in the United States of America in 2018 by Kane Press, Inc.
Printed in China

Book Design and Photograph/Image Research: Maura Taboubi

Visit us online at www.kanepress.com.

Like us on Facebook
facebook.com/kanepress

Follow us on Twitter
@KanePress

On Election Day, Americans vote for the people we want to govern our country.

For over two hundred years we have come closer and closer to having "universal suffrage." This means that almost all adults now have the right to become citizens and to vote.

We work hard to make sure our elections are free, fair, honest, and open. But the American path toward universal suffrage has been a long and bumpy one!

Washington speaks after being sworn in as president, 1789.

Timeline: Expanding Voting Rights in America

In 1776, people in the 13 American colonies declared their independence. They wanted to choose their own leaders. So they fought for freedom from the king of England—and won!

The first federal election was completed in January 1789. States set their own rules for voting. In most states, only white, male Protestant property-owners over the age of 21 were allowed to vote. So only about 1% of the population actually voted!

Over time, the laws about who could vote began to change.

By 1828, there were no more religious restrictions on voting.

By 1856, *all* white men over 21 were allowed to vote—not just property owners.

"Scene at the Polls," the presidential election of 1856

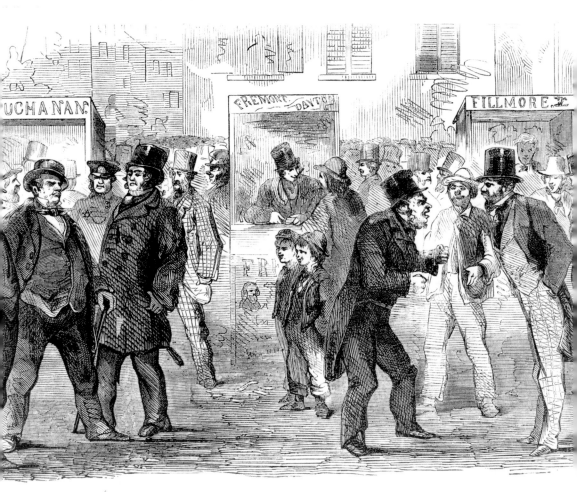

After the Civil War, all the slaves were freed. And in 1870, the right to vote was given to African American men.

Two African American men were elected as Senators. But whites soon took actions that made it hard for both African Americans and poor whites to vote:

- People had to pay *poll taxes* before they could vote. Many did not have the money.
- People had to take *literacy tests*. The tests were extremely difficult to pass.
- African Americans had to deal with *threats of violence*. These threats scared many away from voting.

Hiram Revels (left) of Mississippi became the first African American Senator in 1870. Five years later, Blanche K. Bruce (right) of Mississippi became the second.

Former slaves vote in New Orleans.

As a result, the number of African American men registered to vote in the South dropped to less than 6%!

Five thousand women gathered at the Capitol in 1914 to demand voting rights.

In 1932, Hattie Wyatt Caraway of Arkansas became the first woman elected to the U.S. Senate.

In 1920, American women finally won the right to vote when the 19th Amendment to the Constitution passed. Women had fought tirelessly for this right for 144 years!

For a long time, Native Americans could not vote. They were forced to choose between being U.S. citizens and being members of their own tribes. But in 1924, all Native Americans were allowed to become U.S. citizens. Some states allowed them to vote. Some did not.

Native Americans with U.S. officials, 1891

In 1907, Charles Curtis (right) of Kansas and Robert Owen of Oklahoma became the first U.S. Senators of Native American descent.

In 1943, the Chinese Exclusion Act was repealed. For over 60 years, Chinese laborers had been prevented from immigrating to the U.S. Now they could immigrate, become citizens, and vote.

In 1946, immigrants from India were allowed to become citizens and vote.

Hiram Fong from Hawaii became the first Chinese American Senator in 1959.

A laborer on the street in Chinatown, San Francisco

A Japanese nurse for the U.S. Navy, 1943. Despite nursing for
the U.S. military, she could not yet become a citizen or vote.

By 1947, all the states had granted the right
to vote to Native Americans.

In 1952, Japanese Americans who were born
in the U.S. were allowed to become citizens
and vote.

The Civil Rights Movement of the 1950s and 1960s caused huge changes in U.S. voting laws. African Americans had the *right* to vote but too often were not allowed to *use* that right!

A turning point came in 1965. Hundreds of people gathered in Alabama to march from Selma to Montgomery. They were protesting how difficult it was for African Americans to register to vote.

New Yorkers (below) and people in other cities formed their own marches to support the marchers in Selma.

The first two attempts at the march were met with police violence. So the president sent in National Guard troops to protect the marchers.

The third attempt was successful. By then, 25,000 people had joined the 50-mile march.

The result of the protest was that Congress passed the Voting Rights Act. It no longer allowed unfair practices that kept African Americans or poor whites from registering or voting.

The civil rights march from Selma to Montgomery, 1965

Men as young as 18 years old fought in the Vietnam War.

In 1971, the voting age was lowered from 21 to 18. This happened because of the Vietnam War. Supporters said that if people are old enough to fight, they are old enough to vote.

In 1975, Congress expanded the Voting Rights Act. Voting information would now be translated into Spanish and other languages for those who needed help reading English. As a result, more Americans were able to vote.

By 1975, voting information was translated into other languages.

POLLING PLACE
★ VOTE HERE ★
CENTRO DE VOTACIÓN
VOTE AQUÍ

But voting rights have not always been *expanded*. Sometimes they have been *restricted*.

This happened in 2000 to the residents of Puerto Rico, Guam, American Samoa, and the U.S. Virgin Islands. A federal court ruled that the 4 million people living in U.S. colonies cannot vote in presidential elections, even though they are U.S. citizens.

Today Americans are still working to make sure that everyone who has the *right* to vote is registered and can actually *use* that right.

A young girl waves an American flag at a celebration in Puerto Rico.

People running for office often go into their communities to meet voters before the election.

Preparing to Vote

Voting is a privilege, but it is also a big responsibility. We protect our freedoms in America by trying to elect wise and honest leaders. We also protect our freedoms by voting on issues small and large—from building a new school to changing the Constitution.

- Before we vote, we can learn about the people and the issues on the ballot.
- We can learn about the political parties, their candidates, and their "platforms"—or ideas for improving our government.
- We can read newspapers and voting guides. And we can watch news programs and debates.
- We can talk with people whose opinions are like our own—and with those whose opinions are different!
- We can think about how our votes will affect us *and* our fellow Americans.

We can learn about candidates from many sources, such as newspapers or voting guides.

Registering to Vote

Before we vote for the first time, we must register. In more and more states, registration is automatic whenever we get a driver's license or ID card. In North Dakota, people don't have to register at all. They just bring IDs and vote!

In other states, we still must register in person, by mail, or online. We first need to show an ID card. Then we fill out a form. This usually must be done well ahead of the election.

A young woman registers to vote.

Polling places are often located in public buildings like schools or government offices.

When Are Elections Held?

General Election Day is held in even-numbered years. It is the first Tuesday after the first Monday in November.

We have a presidential election every four years.

In between those years, also in even-numbered years, we have "midterm elections." These elections are very important, too. Even though we don't vote for a president, we vote for many other leaders and issues.

Top: The U.S. Capitol, home of Congress
Above: The state Capitol in West Virginia
Right: City Hall in Kansas City

There are three levels of elections in the
United States: federal, state, and local.

The president works in the White House's Oval Office.

Federal Elections

We select members of two of the three branches of the federal government on General Election Day.

- **The Executive Branch:** We vote for a president and vice president.
- **The Legislative Branch:** We vote for members of Congress. Senators are elected for six-year terms. Representatives are elected for two-year terms.
- **The Judicial Branch:** We do not vote for federal judges. The president nominates Supreme Court justices and other federal judges. They must all be approved by the Senate.

State Elections

- We vote for state officials such as the governor, who runs a state's government.
- We elect people to represent us in the state's law-making body, the state legislature.
- We also elect most state justices and judges.
- We vote on issues such as raising the minimum wage for workers in our state.

Left: A state voting guide for California
Below: The governor's office, Oregon

A county sheriff with a police dog at a fair in Colorado

Local Elections

- We vote for local officials such as the city mayor or the county sheriff.
- We vote for members of groups such as the school board or the city council.
- Many local judges are appointed by the governor or the state legislature. But some local judges are elected.
- We vote on projects we are being asked to pay for—such as buying a new fire truck.

How We Vote

Each state decides how its people vote. Many states set up special places to vote called "polling places." People arrive on Election Day, get in line, and wait for their turn to vote.

A few states have all their voters send in their votes by mail.

People can vote at a polling place or by mail.

OFFICIAL ELECTION BALLOT

VOTE & RETURN PROMPTLY

CONTAINS VOTE ON PROPOSED TAX INCREASE

vote!

All states have "secret ballots." This means that no one can see how anybody else voted. People vote on paper ballots or use voting machines.

Most states also allow early voting—ahead of Election Day. The goal is to get as many people as possible to vote.

The larger the number of people who vote, the more the election represents all of the people!

People vote on paper ballots or use voting machines.

A Big Election Day Problem

A big problem we have on Election Day is low voter turnout. This means that many people don't show up to vote.

About 60% of qualified people actually vote in presidential elections. Only about 40% vote in midterm elections. And only 20% of young people (aged 18–25) cast votes!

In 2016, less than 30% of qualified people elected the president.

A nearly empty polling place

Elections can be decided by very few votes. In the 2000 presidential election, 537 votes out of almost 6 million votes cast actually decided the election.

Many people have tried to figure out why voter turnout is so low in the U.S. There are a number of possible reasons.

- In some states, it can *still* be difficult to register and to vote.
- Some polling places have shortened the hours they are open. This is discouraging to voters.
- People are frustrated by long lines at polling places.
- It is not always easy to find time to vote on a Tuesday, in the middle of the work week.
- Some people think, "My vote won't make a difference." But every vote matters!

Voting on General Election Day

Celebrating General Election Day

In eight states, General Election Day is a civic holiday. But all of us can still celebrate Election Day, whether or not it's a holiday, and whether or not we are old enough to vote.

- First and foremost, we can remind all the adults we know to vote!
- We can help neighbors who don't have transportation find a way to vote.
- When we see people wearing "I voted!" stickers, we can thank them for voting.
- We can join in the excitement as we watch the election results roll in.

Whether our favorite candidates win or lose, we will have the satisfaction of knowing we have done our part in protecting our democracy.

A crowd gathers to see the inauguration.

The White House

Americans are very lucky to have a democratic system where elections are, for the most part, fair and honest.

But not everyone in the world has this privilege. In some countries, people have no voice in their government. The leaders have complete power over their people. And these leaders often rule for a long, long time.

Above: Abraham Lincoln being sworn in as president
Left: A poster encouraging people to vote

People around the world watch democratic countries like ours. They want to see how a democracy works. They want to see if we use our freedoms responsibly.

Voting in elections gives us a voice in our government. And the more people who vote—people of all genders, races, colors, and religions—the more the results reflect the wishes of all Americans.

We can use our voices to make America stronger, safer, kinder, and more generous.

We can help to make America a good place for ALL Americans . . . and a good neighbor to the rest of the world.

A boy and his mother wave an American flag at a parade in Washington, D.C.